BRITISH-BUILT BUSES ABROAD IN THE 1980s

MIKE RHODES

AMBERLEY

First published 2019

Amberley Publishing
The Hill, Stroud
Gloucestershire, GL5 4EP

www.amberley-books.com

ISBN 978 1 4456 9020 9 (print)
ISBN 978 1 4456 9021 6 (ebook)

British Library Cataloguing in Publication Data.
A catalogue record for this book is available from the British Library.

Orgination by Amberley Publishing.
Printed in the UK.

Introduction

At one time Britain led the way in the manufacture and supply of buses to all corners of the world, just as it had done in the days of railway mania in the latter half of the nineteenth century. Even as early as 1911 Leyland Motors sold five single-deck charabancs to Lisbon Tramways and three to Cape Town Electric Tramways. As Leyland continued to develop its product range in the 1920s, examples of its A13 model were exported to Calcutta, Dunedin Corporation in New Zealand and Kowloon Motor Bus (KMB) in Hong Kong. KMB also received three Leyland Lions in 1926, as did China Motor Bus (CMB), along with a number of operators in South Africa who also took small numbers of the type. The link between Leyland and South Africa continued to be exploited as both Cape Town Tramways and Durban Corporation Transport trialled their first double-decker buses in 1928. Two years later two TD1s were exported to India while another twelve went half way around the world to Australia, where they were used by a number of Antipodean operators. The connections which Leyland forged in the early development of its bus range would stand the company in good stead following the end of the Second World War.

Large numbers of Leyland's post-war Titan range were sold to a number of operators in India, South Africa and Australia, with the Sydney Department of Government Transport taking a significant number of the OPD1 and OPD2 chassis marques. These were part of a combined order for 845 chassis from AEC, Albion Motors and Leyland. The bodies were constructed by two local coachbuilders. Leyland's PD1 double-decker model was also operated by both the Lisbon and Madrid municipalities. While the former later standardised on AEC products, the latter purchased a significant number of MCCW-bodied OPD2/6s. Meanwhile, the single-deck overseas version, the OPS range, was exported in large numbers to a wide range of operators in South Africa. As Leyland developed its range of underfloor and rear-engined buses in the 1950s and 1960s, both the Olympic and Worldmaster found favour across the globe.

The early version of the Olympic, produced from 1950 onwards, was sold in a number of South American countries, particularly Argentina and Uruguay, while later versions went to operators in Cuba, Jamaica, South Africa and Turkey. The Royal Tiger Worldmaster was sold overseas in its thousands, with more than 5,000 seeing service in Israel alone. They were also to be seen in large numbers in Central America, the Caribbean and across Europe. The links that Leyland had forged with operators for the supply of double-deckers continued into the 1960s and 1970s as the Atlantean was exported to a number of overseas operators, most notably to the municipalities of Baghdad, Pretoria, Oporto, Singapore, Stockholm and Tehran. Closer to home, the Dutch market was also of some significance as both the Worldmaster and later the National were enthusiastically received in the Netherlands.

Among the many customers of the Leyland Titan had been several of the large Indian city operators. These included Bombay (Mumbai), Calcutta (Kolkata) and Madras (Chennai). In 1948 Ashok Motors was founded in Madras and later obtained a license to build the Leyland Comet single-decker model. This was followed in 1967 by a version of Leyland's popular PD3 which was known as the ALPD but was akin to the PD3/5 model, having semi-automatic gears and a 0.680 engine. Ashok Motors cornered the Indian market with first the Comet and then the 'Leyland' Viking, with both models selling in their thousands. These buses carried bodies constructed by local coachbuilders such as Antony Motors, Mahindra Owen Ltd and Sion Garage Ltd, all of which were based in Mumbai. Typically the ALPDs would be fitted out with seventy-eight seats although in reality they carried many more standees. The first models were traditional halfcabs but these progressed to a full-fronted version. As recently as 2010–3 Bangladesh took delivery of an order for 290 ALPDs while over a hundred of the type were still in daily service in Mumbai in 2018.

Leyland was not the only player in the overseas market as AEC, Daimler and Guy Motors all had a significant share of the early post-war orders. Daimler's CVG (Victory) range of front-engined double-deckers particularly found favour in Hong Kong with some 665 of the various derivatives joining the KMB fleet between 1949 and 1972; these were then followed by 450 Fleetlines. As London Transport dispensed with its unreliable Fleetlines, in the early 1980s, both CMB and KMB jumped at the opportunity to add more of the type to their expansive fleets. Daimler also had loyal customers in Australia and South Africa; indeed Johannesburg MT took a large order for Daimler Fleetlines during the 1970s before switching to Mercedes. On the other side of Victoria harbour in Hong Kong, CMB assembled a large fleet of Guy Arab single-deckers, many of which were later rebodied as double-deckers in the 1960s and 1970s. Guy Motors was based in Wolverhampton and as early as 1926 it had supplied a large number of its BB single-decker model to Rio de Janeiro. After the war Khartoum Province Public Transport took a number of single-deck Guy Arab IIIs and the East India Transport Co. in Karachi took a batch of Guy Vixens. The Guy name continued to be used sparingly until 1979 as the export model, the Guy Victory, continued to be produced in large numbers; particularly by a variety of operators in South Africa. Having been absorbed by Leyland Motors in 1968, the Guy factory was eventually closed in 1981.

AEC (Associated Equipment Company) was also not to be outdone by its rivals. For many years associated with manufacturing bus chassis for London Transport, AEC also supplied chassis to operators abroad, particularly after the Second World War, with its Regent and Regal ranges. AEC's impressive list of customers included the Australian Department of the Interior (Canberra/Darwin/Tasmania), Baghdad Passenger Transport Services, DSB Copenhagen, Johannesburg MT, Kowloon Motorbus, Teheran Municipal Transport, Sociedade de Transportes Colectivos do Porto (Oporto), West Bengal State Transport (Calcutta), West Pakistan RTC (Karachi/Lahore) and Lisbon Electric Tramways or CARRIS as it became known. The last operator was somewhat significant as a relationship was established with the Portuguese bodybuilder União de Transportadores para Importação e Comércio (UTIC), whereby later batches of chassis to AEC's design were assembled on home soil. Such a franchise was not unusual as we have already seen with Ashok Motors. Along the same lines MCCW established a subsidiary in South Africa which was known as BBA or Busaf (Bus Bodies South Africa). Indeed, while thousands of British-built chassis were exported to Hong Kong a great number of the bodies were constructed by Metal Sections Ltd of Oldbury in the West Midlands or the British Aluminium Company Ltd (BACO) and shipped to the Far East as a kit of parts (completely knocked down) for assembly in the operators' own workshops.

Whereas most buses used by overseas operators were new vehicles, there were a few notable exceptions. As London Transport found itself with a surfeit of serviceable buses in the 1960s, hundreds of redundant RT/RTL/RTWs were snapped up by the Ceylon Transport Board. The total number of buses acquired by the Board exceeded 1,270 and they were used to completely transform the island's bus services. Continuing the London theme, redundant Atlanteans and Daimler Fleetlines found favour with both KMB and CMB while in the region of sixty AEC Swifts saw further service with the Public Transport Association (PTA) and the Education Department on the island of Malta. However, one of the most unusual congregation of second-hand British buses was that of the local operator in the Portuguese colony of Macau, namely Companhia de Autocarros Fok-Lei Limitida. To say the buses Fok Lei acquired were antiquated was an understatement as they comprised mainly Eastern Coach Works-bodied Bristol L5Gs which dated from the period 1939–50 and had already seen a significant amount of front-line service with their original British operators. Many were still in their almost original condition at the start of the 1980s.

The story of British-built buses abroad by no means ends in the 1980s but by then some of the other European bus builders such as MAN, Mercedes, Scania and Volvo had gained a significant share of the market, either through the closure of British manufacturing plants or by the merger with or takeover of others. The last rear-entrance double-decker bus in service to be built in the UK and supplied new to an overseas operator succumbed in July 1984, when KMB withdrew its last Daimler CVG5s. By then all its later Daimler CVGs had been rebuilt as front/centre-entrance vehicles. It says something for the endurance of the British-built chassis when examples of the Daimler CVG in Hong Kong and the AEC Regent III in Lisbon both managed to attain well over twenty-five years of service for their respective operators. Both KMB and CMB continued to buy chassis from Dennis and Leyland well into the 1990s and Alexander Dennis (ADL) was later joined by Wrightbus of Ballymena in Northern Ireland in supplying bus bodies to bus operators throughout the world, which they continued to do as these notes were penned.

Finally, an explanation about the choice of some of the illustrations in relation to the title of the book. By and large most of the pictures included in the following pages depict buses at work in the 1980s. However, some pictures of a more recent nature have also been included, particularly to illustrate buses at work in India and Malta where there is a strong British influence and they can be considered relevant to the era under review. Most of the sixty or so ex-LT Swifts obtained by the MPTA/Education Dept. in the 1980s were still in use on the island well into the twenty-first century. Similarly, the Brihanmumbai Electric Supply & Transport Company (BEST) was still running buses in Mumbai that had been built by Ashok Leyland in the 1990s but were of a basic design which had hardly changed since the late 1960s or 1970s. I hope the reader enjoys dipping in to this publication to learn about the wide range of buses which could be found plying the thoroughfares of such diverse places as Lantau Island in the Far East and San Francisco's central district in the United States during the latter days of the British influence abroad.

Mike Rhodes
March 2019

Prior to 1962 China Motor Bus (CMB) had only been permitted to operate single-deck buses due to the hilly nature of some of the routes. The company had been an early exponent of the Guy Arab and embarked on a programme of rebodying a number of former single-deck buses with Metal Sections double-deck bodies between 1973 and 1975. Arab V No. LS27 (low height/short wheelbase) is seen in Shau Kei Wan Road in October 1981.

In the early 1980s CMB purchased a bewildering array of different types of buses in order to test the market. The MB class was an 11.5-metre-long MCW-bodied Metrobus with CMB taking a solitary example in December 1978. This was followed by a further thirty-nine production models in 1979. No. MB38 is seen in Nathan Road, on the Kowloon mainland, working one of the cross-harbour tunnel routes to Shau Kei Wan.

No. M18 was a medium wheelbase Met. Sec-bodied Guy Arab V. These sixty-eight-seat front-entrance buses were obtained during the period 1969–71 and were powered by a Gardner 6LX engine for use on the hilly routes (denoted by the white-painted radiator). No. M18 is seen emerging from Belcher's Street at Kennedy Town on route 77 from nearby West Point to Aberdeen. It was withdrawn in June 1982.

There is a marked contrast in body styles on these two CMB vehicles, which have just left North Point bus station. On the left is (long) Daimler Fleetline No. LF52 with a H102D Metal Sections body, while alongside is Alexander-bodied Dennis Jubliant No. DS8, also with a capacity of 102 seated passengers. The former dates from 1975 while the latter entered service in February 1980.

This is a view of CMB's Aberdeen garage as seen from the Ap Lei Chau road bridge. There are forty-four buses in this picture. Nearest the camera is Alexander rebodied Guy Arab V No. LX277 while just visible, up against the building wall, is the roof of derelict former Southdown Guy Arab IV No. MW7. See the picture below to see how the depot looked ten years later.

The Only Way is Up! By 1990 the open parking lot at Aberdeen had partly been redeveloped and a four-storey multi-level garage built on part of the site. A selection of Alexander-bodied LF and LX types can be seen crammed into what is left of the open yard. The solitary short Guy Arab, alongside the garage wall, would be in use as a service vehicle as the last of the type were withdrawn from PSV use in 1984. (JW)

A close-up view of CMB No. MW7, former Southdown Motors No. 554. A Park Royal-bodied Guy Arab IV, it was one of seventeen of the type which were acquired in 1971. This one has survived in the old red and cream livery which was superseded in the mid-1970s. The front entrance was an addition made by CMB. The batch was withdrawn en bloc in September 1981, although this one obviously hadn't run for some time.

Among CMB's miscellaneous intake of buses in the early 1980s were two 12-metre three-axle Duple Met. Sec-bodied Dennis Condors, numbered DL1/2. No more of the type were taken until 1989, when a further forty-six entered the fleet. No. DL4 is seen at North Point Ferry bus station in November 1990. (JW)

While the S and LS classes were both of equal length at 26 feet, the S type was 5 inches higher at 14 feet 7 inches. The class comprised forty-nine buses and they were again produced by mounting new Metal Sections bodies on former single-deck Guy Arab V chassis. No. S10 is seen picking up a healthy load of passengers in Sai Wan Ho bus station in October 1981. The S class buses were all withdrawn between 1982 and 1984.

In 1979/80 CMB bought a batch of thirty shorter (31 feet) Alexander-bodied Daimler Fleetlines for use mainly on routes 6 and 15. Route 15 followed a winding road part way up the summit of Victoria Peak and the shorter body length was an advantage for negotiating some of the tight bends. No. SF11 has just started its decent of the Peak Road on its way back to Central.

Both CMB and KMB availed themselves of large numbers of London Transport's cast-off Fleetlines. Deemed unsuitable for London's traffic conditions, they performed admirably well in the humid and sticky atmosphere of the Hong Kong climate. CMB took no fewer than 206 of the type between 1980 and 1984. No. XF33 is seen making its way along Praya Kennedy. The dock area to the left has since been reclaimed for redevelopment and the Praya is now called Catchick Street. It is, however, still traversed by HK's distinctive trams.

In the mid-1960s CMB stocked its fleet with large numbers of single-deck Guy Arab Vs. These included forty 35-foot-long buses which became known as Long Dragons. From 1972 onwards the whole batch was rebodied as double-deckers using BACO kits. No. LX114 was constructed in 1975 and gave eleven years' service in this guise. It is seen picking up an enthusiastic group of passengers in Shau Kei Wan bus station in December 1985. (JW)

A number of Guy Arabs went on to enjoy a third existence so to speak. 150 buses, which were mainly drawn from the previously rebodied LX class, were fitted with new eighty-seat Alexander bodies between 1977 and 1985. The class also included a number of former West Midlands PTE bus chassis. No. LX313 is seen reposing at North Point Ferry bus station in December 1985. (JW)

During CMB's scramble to get its hands on as many former British operators' buses as possible, in the early 1970s it acquired London Transport's entire class of fifty Park Royal-bodied Leyland Atlanteans. Retaining the same fleet numbers, they had relatively short lives with CMB. No. XA30 is about to meet an ignominious end at Causeway Bay while former Southdown PD3 No. PD21 (825) skulks in the background.

If Leyland Motors had managed to break into the Far East market, the number of Titan B15s that were manufactured may well have been considerably more than the 1,174 which were actually built. As it happens, CMB tried a solitary example but did not pursue any further orders. No. TC1 was fitted out with seventy-three coach-type seats and spent most of its time on route 260, which ran between Central and Stanley.

Both CMB and KMB used a wide selection of former buses as service vehicles. HK 4196 was a 1954 Guy Arab IV which was converted for use as a towing vehicle and used as such from 1977 to 1983. It was fitted with an 8-foot-wide body following an accident and had retained its exposed radiator. As such it was generally used on route 7B until withdrawal in 1973. It is seen at Aberdeen garage in October 1981.

Among all the ex-British buses acquired by CMB in the 1970s was a large intake of former Southdown Leyland Titans. No. PD506 was a Northern Counties-bodied PD3/5 which was received in April 1975. Originally with a full front, it was converted to a half-cab and fitted with a Gardner 6LX engine in 1984. It is seen in On Yip Street in Chai Wan in December 1985. (JW)

Another small batch of buses registered with CMB were Nos SD1–6. These were 31-foot-long (9.5 metre) Dennis Dominators fitted with ninety-seat low-height (13 feet 8 inches) Alexander bodies, enabling them to be used on route 15. No. SD1 is seen setting out from Central Star Ferry bus station in October 1990, heading for the Peak. (JW)

Continuing with the theme of small classes, there were only two of these MCW-bodied Scania Metropolitans, which entered the fleet in November 1975. No. MS2 is seen at North Point Ferry bus station in December 1985. While No. MS1 was withdrawn in 1987, this particular vehicle lasted a couple of years longer. (JW)

Parking cars fully on the pavement is usually frowned upon in the UK but it was not uncommon to encounter a bus so parked in HK. No. M14 was a medium-wheelbase Metal Sections-bodied Guy Arab V and is seen in the centre of Aberdeen in October 1981. The white radiator signified that the bus was fitted with a Gardner 6LX engine and was therefore suitable to be used on hilly routes, of which there was quite a number around Aberdeen.

No. DM1 was a three-axle H110D Duple Met. Sec-bodied Dennis Condor. CMB operated three classes of the Condor. Besides the 12-metre-long DL class, the fifty-six-strong DA class featured air conditioning (AC) while the twenty-eight members of the DM class were non-AC. The location is the Macau Ferry Terminal bus station in November 1990. (JW)

These two Burlingham-bodied Leyland PD3/4s had certainly done the rounds by the time this picture was taken in 1981. New to Ribble Motor Services of Preston as Nos 1576/59 in 1957, they later operated for Southend Transport while on loan from Ensignbus. CMB acquired four of the type in 1976 and these two became Nos T6 and T5 in the training fleet. They are seen at Causeway Bay, where they were broken up.

Buses out of service snake around the periphery of the Macau Ferry bus station while Kowloon and the New Territories' hills dominate the far distant skyline. Metrobus No. MB16 can be seen on the left while Alexander-bodied Fleetline No. LF211 is parked on the right. (JW)

Former Southdown Northern Counties-bodied Leyland PD3/4 No. PD33 (formerly No. 826) is seen at the Wan Chai Ferry bus terminal in December 1985. Of the original seventy-eight acquired Titans, only Nos PD11 and 33 were converted to half-cab and fitted with Gardner 6LX engines. The last of these buses were withdrawn the following year. (JW)

Although CMB took two examples of the Leyland Olympian in 1981, it would be another ten years before any more of the type joined the fleet – and they would be air conditioned buses. No. BR1 was an ONLXB/1R model with a typical-looking Eastern Coach Works body, except the seating capacity was eighty-nine. No. BR2 was 2 feet longer and seated ten more passengers. It is seen at Chai Wan depot in November 1993. (PG)

Sadly most buses end their days in scrap yards and are cut up into small pieces with the various parts, such as engines and axles sold on, along with the piles of scrap metal. Such was the scene at Chai Wan in December 1985, when former London Fleetline No. XF47, Fleetline No. LF39, Guy Arabs Nos LS56 and LX208 and former Southdown PD3 No. PD510 were awaiting the cutter's torch. The gas canister/acetylene torch and cast-off axle are an indicator of what is about to happen. (JW)

In the early 1970s Leyland Motors stepped up its sales campaign in order to secure more orders overseas. Passenger Transport Services of Baghdad was no stranger to British-built buses having purchased a considerable number of Park Royal-bodied AEC Regent Vs from 1958 to 1967. It looked to the UK again in 1976/7 and ordered 400 dual-door Atlanteans with Park Royal bodies. A further 200, with single doors, followed in 1980/1. Two of the type were in use by Citibus of Gibraltar in 2016. (PG)

Top Deck Travel of Horsell near Woking offered a means of crossing the globe (literally) by bus to under-thirty-fives throughout the 1970s and into the 1990s. The fleet was made up entirely of second-hand Bristols, the vast majority of which were Lodekkas. Virtually the entire fleet carried names and *Rush*, originally Eastern National No. 2875 in October 1966, is seen near Grindlewald in Switzerland in May 1986. *Flange* (JAE 632D, ex-Bristol Omnibus C7292) can be seen in the background. (PG)

Companhia Carris de Ferro de Lisboa (CCFL), or Carris as it is also known, was founded on 18 September 1872, originally to operate trams in the city of Lisbon. Electric trams were introduced in 1901 and an extensive tramway system was established over the ensuing years. It was only during the Second World War that buses began to have any significance and following the cessation of hostilities the operator turned to the UK and AEC in particular to supply it with large numbers of single and double-deck buses.

Comércio Square in Lisbon has been the focal point for the city's bus and tram services for many years. During the 1960s CCFL stocked its fleet with a large number of AEC Regent Vs. They had a mixture of bodywork which included Weymann, CCFL and UTIC-AEC. The livery of the buses had hitherto been green and cream and then dark green with a white band. The change to orange and cream was made in the late 1970s. CCFL-bodied Regent Vs Nos 640 and 716 are seen at the Praça do Comércio in April 1982.

CCFL operated a fleet of fifty-five Daimler CRG Fleetlines. While the majority were fitted with in-house CCFL-constructed bodies, the last five had a more angular appearance. No. 851 had a UTIC body while Nos 852–5 were new in March 1972 and were fitted with seventy-two-seat dual-entrance Salvador Caetano bodies. No. 854 is seen in Rossio Square with CCFL/Regent V No. 604 behind in April 1982. The Fleetline was eventually withdrawn in August 1995.

The CCFL-bodied Daimler Fleetlines were received between 1967 and 1969 and were fitted out with seventy-nine seats. Unlike the last five, they were single-doored buses. Carris had a number of garages which were either shared with the trams or were built exclusively for the buses. One such garage was at Cabo Ruivo, which was opened in December 1958 and was situated in Avenida Marechal Gomes da Costa, where No. 812 is seen over the inspection pits.

In 1967 Carris took delivery of twenty UTIC-bodied Guy Victories. These buses were unusual in that they had three doors and only eighteen seats, being largely designed to accommodate standees. Latterly they were almost exclusively confined to route 15 and No. 79 is seen in Rua das Amoreiras. The arch in the background is part of the Aquaduto das Águas Livres and dates from the mid-eighteenth century.

Two AEC Regent Vs are seen bursting out of Rua da Prata into Comércio Square in April 1982. Although the seventy-three-seat front-entrance bodies on these buses were constructed at three different locations, they were all largely done to the same Weymann design. No. 612 was one of a batch of thirty-five with CCFL bodies which entered service in 1962. It was withdrawn in November 1984.

Lisbon is not short on hills, as evidenced by this view of Regent V No. 669 creating a blue haze from its exhaust as it slogs its way up the Rua da Palmeira in June 1983 on its way to Marvila. No. 669 was classified as a UTIC-AEC and was fitted with a CCFL-constructed body. It entered service in January 1965.

The classic shape of an AEC radiator gives away this bus as being a Regal III. Carris took its first of the type in December 1947 and assembled a sizeable fleet of them over the next few years. No. 143 dates from 1948 and originally had a B20D Weymann-CCFL body. It was rebodied in 1969. Extremely long-lived, it is seen at Bo Serafina in June 1983 at a location which no longer exists as it is now submerged under the Estação de Campolide railway station complex.

CCFL operated some classic bus routes, one of which was the 39 from São Bento to Marvila. This is 1964 CCFL-UTIC Regent No. 665, still in the old green livery, making an umpteen-point turn at the Marvila terminus. Before reaching this point the bus had to squeeze up a narrow section of road bordered by brick buildings. Buses still served this location in 2018 but no longer made this turn in the road.

This nearside view of Guy Victory No. 70 clearly shows the three doors which were integral to its UTIC body. As previously mentioned, UTIC, which is short for União de Transportadores para Importação e Comércio, was a local bus and truck bodybuilder. The bus is seen in Largo do Rato with one of Lisbon's impressive public buildings in the background.

Another view in Comércio Square depicts the old and the new in April 1982. Weymann-bodied AEC Regent III No. 219 was of the classic fifty-six-seat double-deck layout and was new in May 1952, while next to it is ECW-bodied Leyland Olympian demonstrator No. 925, which is almost thirty years its junior. The Olympian only operated for CCFL for just over a year while the Regent was withdrawn in June of the following year.

You could almost be looking at the classic lines of a British operator's Weymann-bodied bus if the entrance wasn't on the wrong side. 1956 Regent III No. 274 is seen outside Santa Apolonia railway station as it follows 1935-built four-wheel tramcar No. 235. While the bus was withdrawn in 1983, No. 235 was rebuilt and modernised and was still operated by Carris in 2018, but renumbered as No. 551.

Carris used a significant number of former PSV buses as service vehicles. Now carrying the number V23, this one had an interesting previous history. In among the large intake of Regents in the early 1950s were a handful of double-deckers which started life as single-deck Regals (it has a Regal badge on the radiator). No. V23 was originally No. 83, which was new in 1948. It was fitted with a new Weymann double-deck body in 1955 and renumbered 234. It later received another new body in 1967. It is seen at Santo Amaro Depot in June 1983.

Besides running the city's bus services, the Lisbon operator also owned a number of coaches for tours and more long-distance work. UTIC-bodied AEC Reliance No. 159 of 1966 is seen alongside Caetano-bodied Magirus Deutz No. 175 at Santo Amaro tram depot/bus overhaul works (opened in 1901). On the right rebodied 1948 AEC Regal III No. 122 is seen squeezing up Travessa do Funil as it approaches the Castle terminus of route 37. In 2018 route 37 ran as the 737 using minibuses. Both pictures date from 1983.

Bus meets tram 1. Comércio Square was always a hive of activity, being where several of the city's bus and tram routes converged. One of CCFL's fifty locally bodied Daimler Fleetlines, No. 824 of 1967 is seen on express service 81 in October 1986. This bus was later converted to open-top and used on city tours, lasting in service until 2005. (JW)

Bus meets tram 2. Weymann-CCFL rebodied 1948 AEC Regal III No. 119 is seen alongside Santa Apolonia station in Rua da Bica do Sapato in June 1983, working on route 13 from Chelas to Bo Serafina. It is passing single-ended tram No. 485, which is actually newer than the bus and is working a special service. The tram lines have since been taken up. No. 141 of the type is preserved in the UK.

In the late 1960s CCFL embarked on a programme of rebodying a number of AEC Regals with sixty-five-seat double-deck bodies. Looking somewhat shabby in the old faded green livery, No. 492 (ex-No. 23 of 1948) is seen on the opposite side of Santa Apolonia station in Avenida Infante Dom Henrique in April 1982. The last of these rebodied Regals were taken out of service the following year.

Very much a UTIC vehicle, this 'Regent V' comprised a CCFL-UTIC body on a UTIC-AEC chassis and was new in February 1965. No. 673 is seen alongside the monastery at Belem in Rua dos Jerónimos in May 1982. The monastery was finally completed in 1601, with construction work having started 100 years earlier.

In pairs 1. UTIC rebodied AEC Regal No. 481 and AEC Regent III No. 227 pose together at Comércio Square. Only four years separate the build dates of the chassis, which were new in 1948 and 1952 respectively. As Carris bought large numbers of MAN single-deckers between 1982 and 1984, these venerable machines were consigned to history.

In pairs 2. Seen under the shadow of the Águas Livre viaduct are rebodied AEC Regals Nos 123 and 140, waiting to depart Bo Serafina on routes 13 and 20 respectively. Along with route 37, these two routes were still the preserve of the Regals in 1982. While No. 123 has lost its AEC motif, both buses are still sporting their 'Regal' name badges.

Apart from the fact that the bus has long since been scrapped, it would not be possible to capture this scene in 2018 as the photographer would be standing in the middle of a busy six-lane dual carriageway. Rebodied Regal No. 485 has paused opposite Cabo Ruivo depot in Avenida Marechal Gomes da Costa for a crew change on its way to the north-eastern district of Prior Velho. These old buses were still working on route 25 from Comércio Square in 1982.

Regal No. 105 (having previously carried the numbers 57 and 78) was one of five of the 1948 buses which were rebodied by UTIC in 1972, when originally only fifteen seats were provided. Working duty number four on service 20, it is seen carrying a healthy load of mainly seated passengers at Estrela in the west of the city. This locality was still served by the old refurbished four-wheel trams on line 25 in 2018.

No. 321 was new in 1958 and, along with No. 323, it was one of the last Regent Vs to be received with an open-platform rear entrance. It is seen in the Santa Amaro depot complex in April 1982 only a few weeks before it was withdrawn. In the background can be seen the concrete bridge supports for the Ponte 25 de Abril Bridge (opened in 1966) which spans the adjacent River Tagus.

Daimler Fleetline No. 851 was the odd one out of the last five of the type in as much as its body was constructed by UTIC as opposed to Caetano. New in 1972, Nos 851–5 were the last buses with a British influence to be bought by Carris. The original order had actually been for thirty chassis. It is seen in Comercio Square in October 1986. No. 851 has been spared the cutter's torch and is now preserved in the Carris Museum of Transport. (JW)

Macau remained a Portuguese colony until 1999. Between 1956 and 1966 the principal bus operator, Companhia de Autocarros Fok Lei Limitida (CAFL), which was established in 1948, assembled a fascinating collection of former British operators' ECW-bodied Bristol L5Gs, the oldest of which dated from 1939. No. L112 was new to Southern National as No. 338 in 1939 and passed to CAFL in 1962. Other than being converted to B33D, it was almost in original condition when seen in Rua do Campo in October 1981.

At least three former Bolton Corporation buses saw out their existence in Macau, including this East Lancashire-bodied Leyland PD3A. No. 172 in the Bolton fleet, it still retained much of its original body shape although it has gained a centre entrance and full-depth sliding windows. No. 211 in the CAFL fleet, it is working route 11, which crossed the 8,431-foot-long Taipa Bridge, opened in October 1974, and joined the smaller island of Taipa to Macau. Having been superseded by two other bridges, it now only conveys buses and taxis.

CAFL also obtained a number of Bristol LS5Gs from former British operators. This is former Bristol Omnibus No. 2848, one of four that came from that operator, which was new in 1954 and joined the CAFL fleet as No. LS136 in 1971. It was initially fitted with two extra doors before being further modified as shown above. It is seen on service 2 in the centre of Macau.

In total CAFL operated thirty Bristol L5Gs, eight of which had been new to Bristol Tramways, the former name of the Bristol Omnibus Co. No. L119 dated from 1947 and was one of eight of the type which had operated for the Tramways fleet, as No. 2717. It is seen in Avenida de Almeida Ribeiro working on service 5. This section of road was largely unaltered in 2018 although the bus services were in the hands of three main operators, including Transportes Urbanos de Macau, the former CAFL.

The traditional Eastern Coach Works bodies were gradually replaced by locally built bodies constructed by Sun Cheong of Hong Kong. No. L111 started out as Western National No. 325 in 1939. It passed to a dealer in Stratford, E15, in 1959 who sold it on to CAFL. It was converted to B33D in 1976 and rebodied a few years later. It is seen on the outskirts of Macau in October 1981.

CAFL 1954 ECW–bodied Bristol LS5G No. LS131 was originally United Automobile No. BU37. It was acquired by Fok Lei from dealer W. North in August 1969 and converted to B41D. It is seen in Macau bus station in Rua do Visconde Paco de Arcos. In 1981 the bus station was situated alongside Ponte (Jetty) 16, which was still standing in 2018 but by then the forecourt no longer functioned as a bus station.

Seen in the bus station in December 1985 are ECW-bodied Bristol KSW6G M-07-15 and East Lancs-bodied Daimler CVG6 M-87-56. The KSW was one of a pair which originally ran for Bristol Omnibus, having carried the number C8426. Similarly, CAFL also acquired two Daimlers from Bolton Corporation, this one formerly being No. 143 in the Lancashire fleet. CAFL's collection of double-deckers also included buses which previously operated for United Counties, Mansfield District, Southern Vectis, Ribble Motors and Yorkshire Traction. (JW)

Another very recently rebodied Bristol L5G by Sun Cheong was No. L117, which is seen in Rua do Visconde Paco de Arcos. This was originally new in 1947 as Eastern Counties No. LL648. It was exported to Macau in 1964 and modified to dual entrance. The L5Gs underwent an intense rebodying programme between 1981 and 1983.

Bristol L5G No. L113 was the recipient of a new B29D body constructed by Metro Dodwell in 1975, which saw it retain its original radiator. Originally West Yorkshire Roadcar No. 184, it was new in March 1940 and exported to Macau in 1956. As previously mentioned, the building in the background was still standing in 2018 but was completely overshadowed by a new gargantuan plush hotel, just to the right.

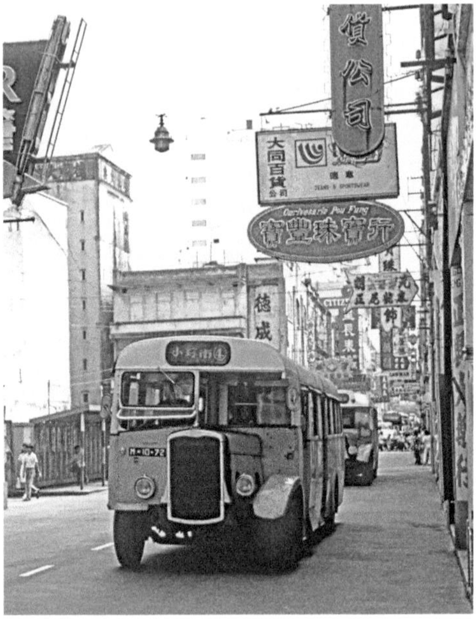

Two views taken in Avenida de Almeida Ribeiro. On the left is former Southern Vectis No. 501, which dated from 1954 and was converted to open-top format after arriving in Macau in the mid-1970s. The picture on the right depicts L5G No. L103, which dated from 1939 and was formerly Eastern Counties No. LL47, and equally old No. L102, which started out as West Yorkshire Roadcar No. 152. Neither bus survived long enough to be included in the rebodying programme.

Such has been the redevelopment in Macau over the last thirty-seven years that the author has been unable to establish where this location is (or was). Seen at a busy crossroads served by routes 1, 3 and 5 is Bristol L5G No. L126, which was new in 1949 to United Automobile as No. BLO386. It was converted to B33D in 1965 and rebodied by Sun Cheong by 1983.

Seen at the same location is this 1975 Union Auto-bodied B43D Albion (Leyland) Viking. Albion Motors was based in Scotstoun in Glasgow and from 1951 it was a subsidiary of Leyland Motors. The Viking model was constructed at the Glasgow works from 1963 to 1980, when the works was closed. Most of the type were sold to overseas operators and were badged as Leylands.

A rear view of Bristol LS5G No. LS136, former Bristol Omnibus Co. No. 2848. This was one of four ex-BOC LS5Gs in the CAFL fleet in October 1981. Alongside is 1981-built Albion Viking MA-69-74, which has been bodied by local coachbuilder Sun Cheong. Aesthetically this later style of bodywork was a vast improvement on the style used on some of the earlier rebodied Bristol L5Gs.

The Cape Electric Tramways Co. Ltd was formed in London in July 1897. The first buses joined the City Tramways (as it became known) fleet in 1911. Buses operated throughout the 1930s to 1960s were predominantly Daimlers and Leylands. Large numbers of both single and double-deck Guy (Leyland) Victories joined the fleet from 1973 to 1978. BBA-bodied Guys Nos 1785 and 1761, both from Maitland depot, are seen in Newmarket Street in the centre of Cape Town in November 1982.

City Tramways also operated a number of Leyland PD3/5s. These seventy-two-seater buses were also bodied by BBA and were new from 1962 to 1968. They were very similar in appearance to the Metro-Cammell-bodied PD3As to be found in a number of fleets in the UK, which was not a coincidence as BBA (Bus Bodies SA), later known as Busaf, was established in Port Elizabeth in 1946 as a subsidiary of Metro-Cammell Weymann. No. 279, of 1968, is seen in Cape Town's Golden Acre bus station.

Single-deck Guy Victory No. 1044 was new to the City Tramways fleet in September 1971 and was fitted with a fifty-eight-seat BBA body. It was also licensed to carry eighteen standees. The depot code is shown as a prefix to the number, which in this case is T for Toll Gate. Note how the logo comprises CTL for City Tramways Ltd. The location is Adderley Street in Cape Town city centre. No. 1044 was withdrawn in 1988.

Despite the Leyland badge displayed on the front of CT No. 2000, this one-off Victory was a product of Dennis (as evidenced by the maker's plate behind the door). When originally built in 1979, it took the concept of a standee bus to a whole new level and had no seats at all on the lower deck. However when captured in 1982, seats had been fitted downstairs. It is also of a shorter length than the Guy Victories, having a shorter overhang behind the rear wheels.

Port Elizabeth Tramways (PET) was formed in 1879 and later became a subsidiary of Cape Town Tramways. Vehicles were often swapped between the two companies. PET BBA-bodied 1963 Leyland PD3/5 No. 30 was previously CT No. 189 and had only been in Port Elizabeth for a couple of months when it was captured in Govan Mbeki Avenue (née Main Street) in November 1982. It is still displaying its former CT depot code of K, which indicated Klipfontein Road.

BBA didn't have a complete monopoly with regards to bus body construction in South Africa. Both CT and PET later opened their own factories which constructed bodies under the name of Tours & Services Ltd. PET No. 210 was a Leyland Victory Mk 2 and had its body constructed in the Port Elizabeth factory and was only a few months old when photographed in the depot in November 1982.

City Tramways No. 1257 was a Guy (Leyland) Victory which was fitted with a Tours & Services Ltd Cape Town-built body. This particular bus was new in 1980 and is fitted with a roof luggage rack for the longer distance inter-town services which CT undertook around the Southern Cape area. It is seen in Newmarket Street, alongside Cape Town railway station.

Seen in the bus station at Port Elizabeth, this is 1971 BBA-bodied fifty-eight-seater Guy Victory J No. 914. This bus is recorded as having been transferred to the Southern Cape Passenger Transport Co. Ltd (managed by PET) in January 1981, but clearly this was not the case as it was still working for PET in November of that year. At the time the bus station was located underneath the Settlers Highway flyover.

Seven Guy Victories, all in advert liveries, are seen in Newmarket Street in the centre of Cape Town. Rather than return the buses to the depot between the peak periods, they were parked up close to the railway station, ready to form evening peak hour extras. The majority of the Guys survived with CT until they were transferred to Golden Arrow Bus Services Ltd in April 1992 following the collapse of the Tollgate Group, owners of CT.

Another former CT Leyland PD3/5 is seen in the dark and dingy Port Elizabeth bus station. Displaying what must be some of the largest fleet numerals applied to any bus, No. 144 had previously been No. 152 in the CT fleet. Delivered to Cape Tramways in June 1963, it was extremely long lived, not being withdrawn until April 1990, giving it the honour, along with Nos 708/12, of being the last of the type in service with PET.

Looking very much like a Leyland PS1 or PS2, PET No. 633 is most likely an OPS4/5, Leyland's final overseas equivalent, which was built for the export market between 1954 and 1968. Most likely dating from the mid-1960s, it may also have been rebodied by BBA in the 1970s. It is seen in Port Elizabeth bus station in November 1982.

Both CT and PET operated a number of RT family buses which were acquired from London Transport in the mid to late 1960s. The former RT2604 joined the PET fleet in August 1964 as No. 194. It was repainted LT red in April 1971 for a special shoppers' service but was withdrawn at the end of the year. It had survived as a museum candidate and is seen along with PET 1946 Weymann-bodied Daimler CVG6 CB7723 (No. 1) in the Port Elizabeth garage.

As the production of new buses resumed after the war, in 1946 City Tramways purchased a number of Daimler CVG6s and Leyland PD2/3s. The all-Leyland Titans dated from 1948/9 but were withdrawn by CT in the mid-1960s. This unidentified example has been a remarkable survivor and was encountered in November 1982 on a farm at a small hamlet called Three Sisters, which is situated midway between Bloemfontein and Cape Town.

No. 331 in the Johannesburg MT fleet was unique. Introduced in January 1970, it was a dual-door Park Royal-bodied Daimler Fleetline. It was tagged onto an order made by the West Midlands PTE and was constructed to exactly the same specification. It was obviously considered to be a success as a further 139 of the type, with single-door BBA bodies, were bought between 1971 and 1976. It is seen in Loveday Street in November 1982.

The Johannesburg Municipal Transport fleet livery was an attractive red and white combination but many buses carried all-over advert schemes. No. 384 was one of a large batch of BBA-bodied Daimler CRGs/Leyland FEs which entered the fleet throughout the 1970s. JMT also standardised on Mercedes buses and amassed a large fleet of both single and double-deckers. No. 384 is seen in Kerk Street in November 1982.

Although this book concentrates on buses, there was a small number of operators who still operated British-built trolleybuses in the 1980s, and they could still be found in Johannesburg. These were mainly Guy Sunbeam or Leyland/BUT models; No. 1673 was one of the latter and was new in September 1958. It was fitted with a H73D BBA-built body and is seen in Loveday Street in the centre of the legislative capital of SA in November 1982. The last remnants of the system finally closed in January 1986.

Pretoria City Transport bought a large number of Leyland's ER2/44 Olympic model buses between 1957 and 1970. These sleek-looking vehicles were all bodied by BBA and, other than seven dual-purpose examples bought in 1963, they were all dual-door. No. 12 was one of the first batch of thirty obtained in 1957 and is seen in a deserted Church Square in the centre of Pretoria on a Sunday afternoon in October 1982.

Also seen in Church Square is Olympic No. 455, which was one of the last batch, received in 1970. Over the intervening thirteen years the body style has remained largely unaltered. The BBA bodies were fitted out with either fifty or fifty-one seats. The registration marque TP denotes Transvaal Pretoria. Parked up behind is Scania No. 651 with bodywork which resembled the MCW Metro Scanias seen in some UK fleets.

Several South African towns originally based their fleets on British-built models. Pietermaritzburg Municipality fell in to this group. Post-war, it bought Daimlers and AECs before changing to Leylands and in particular the Leyland Kudu – a South African variant of the AEC/Leyland Regal VI which was an export-only model. However, when Leyland discontinued this model Pietermaritzburg bought Royal Tiger Worldmasters, fifty in total during the 1970s. Busaf/BBA-bodied Nos NPC74 and 80 are seen in the bus station in November 1982. At this time PM also operated MAN, Nissan and Mercedes buses.

Situated some 99 miles to the west of Bloemfontein in the Northern Cape Province is the well-known town of Kimberley, famous for its diamond mines. S A Transport of Kimberley No. 118 was a 1980 forty-five-seat BBA/Busaf-bodied Leyland Victory 2 and is seen in Stanley Street, near the Market Square, in November 1982. By 2018 the white building beyond the trees had been demolished.

The Southern Cape Passenger Transport Company was administered by Port Elizabeth Tramways and as such it was not uncommon to transfer buses between the two. Former PET Leyland OPS4/5 No. 676 and Guy Victory J No. 872, both of which were bodied by BBA/Busaf, await departure from George bus station in November 1982.

Since the late nineteenth century Durban Corporation has operated horse-drawn trams, electric trams, trolleybuses and motorbuses. The first buses were three petrol-engined Thornycroft single-deckers, bought in 1925. Meanwhile, the last trolleybuses ran in March 1968. Durban Corporation was one of the largest bus operators in South Africa and Leyland Worldmaster NDC No. 2060, seen in Dr Pixley Kaseme Street (neé West Street), was representative of the fleet in 1982. The Natural History Museum is on the left.

In 1955 City Tramways of Cape Town bought a number of Leyland's ER44 Olympic series models. They were forty-nine-seaters bodied by BBA/Busaf and lasted in service until the mid-1970s. Reregistered former CT No. 343 is seen at the railway town of Beaufort West, some 270 miles to the east of Cape Town, looking a bit battered but still in use as a PSV.

In January 1933 the Hong Kong Government awarded the franchise to Kowloon Motor Bus Co. (1933) Ltd, or KMB as it became known, to operate bus services on the Kowloon Peninsula and in the New Territories. Only single-deck buses were operated until 1949, after which KMB embarked on the procurement of a large number of Daimler CVGs, many of which survived into the 1980s. Originally buses were identified by their registration marques only and fleet numbers were not introduced until May 1974.

Two AEC Regent Vs and a Daimler CVG6 are seen at Jordan Road bus station. While most of KMB's buses were OPO by 1981, these Regents were still crew-operated, although the conductor was seated behind the front entrance while the rear entrance was for alighting only. This livery style was only applied to the crew-operated Regents.

KMB purchased the first thirty of an eventual 210 AEC Regent Vs in 1963. These buses were larger than any of the type operated in the UK. The initial batch had bodies supplied by the British Aluminium Co. (BACO) while the remainder were fitted with CKD Metal Sections bodies. 1965-built No. A102 is seen in Nathan Road in October 1981.

1962-built Daimler CVG6 No. (D)284 is seen at Hung Hom railway station in October 1981. Nos D261–330 were the first 30 foot by 8-foot-wide buses to be obtained by KMB. They were fitted with Metal Sections bodies and originally had an open-platform rear entrance. Later rebuilt to front and centre-entrance, the seating was also increased from sixty-eight to seventy-five.

In the early 1980s KMB obtained a number of different types of buses to test the market. Four Dennis Jubilants were introduced in 1977/8 which were fitted with KMB's own bodywork. No. N2 is seen at Hung Hom Lower bus station taking on board a group of school children. KMB went on to operate a further 360 of the type.

By the 1980s, the single-deckers operated by KMB were generally to be found operating on a network of routes in the New Territories. Nos L220–69 were Metal Sections-bodied Albion Vikings introduced in 1970/71. No. L257 is about to cross the Kowloon to Canton railway in Sheung Shui, working on direct route 76 to Un Long West (note the garage code U). The railway has since been reconstructed and is now part of the HK MTR system and this road crossing no longer exists.

Buses don't come much squarer looking than this. Following on from the Daimler CVGs, KMB then stocked the fleet with 450 Fleetlines over a four-year period. While most of them carried Met. Sec. bodies, quite a number were fitted with these box-like BACO bodies. No. D1062 is seen in Salisbury Road.

Another four of the type are seen in Tai Kok Tsui Ferry bus station. Nos D1083/13/12 can be clearly identified, all of which are working on route 44A to the Cheung Ching estate, situated on the small island of Tsing Yi. This bus station, along with Jordan Road Ferry bus station, disappeared from the map following the extensive redevelopment of the western coast line in connection with the construction of the new international airport at Lantau.

Following the trial of four Leyland (Guy) Victory buses that were introduced in 1976, KMB proceeded to take a further 539 production models between 1978 and 1983. These were completed with bodies built by W. Alexander which were shipped to Hong Kong CKD for assembly. GV Mk II No. G258 is seen in Nathan Road in October 1982 and was less than twelve months old at the time. Very few KMB buses carried all-over advert schemes at this time.

These diminutive single-deckers were Met. Sec-bodied Albion Chieftains and contained around forty seats. No. L189 was one of a batch of thirty-four which entered service in 1965 and is seen sixteen years later in Po Heung Street in what used to be the market town of Tai Po. Like many of the New Territory locations featured in this book, it has changed out of all recognition in the twenty-first century.

The first 100 Albion Victors entered service in 1961 and were largely based in the New Territories. These two-door buses originally had forty-one seats but were later reduced to thirty-seven in favour of more standees. No. L6 is seen in Kik Yeung Road having just left Yuen (Un) Long West bus station bound for Tai Po Market on route 64. The last three of the batch survived until 1987.

Former London Transport buses tended to find their way to all corners of the world and both CMB and KMB took their fair share of redundant Fleetlines. No. 2D27 (ex-LT DMS727) was one of exactly 100 CRL6s which saw service with KMB between 1981 and 1989. It is seen approaching Jordan Road Ferry bus station on route 4A from Tui Hang Tung. 1964 AEC Regent V No. A41 is in hot pursuit.

The Star Ferry bus station is situated outside the site of the former Kowloon–Canton railway station and has retained a similar layout for many years. In this October 1981 view 1966 AEC Regent V No. A151 and 1976 Daimler Fleetline No. D814 bask in the warm sunshine. Both buses carried bodies which were manufactured by Metal Sections of Oldbury in the UK and shipped out to HK as a kit of parts. Route 6 to Lai Chi Kok was still using the same bus stand in 2018.

Consecutively numbered Daimler CRG6LXBs Nos D965/6 are seen at Jordan Road Ferry bus station. All-over advert buses in the KMB fleet were not as common as might have been expected. These Met. Sec-bodied buses had a seating capacity of over 100. This high capacity was achieved by using a 3+2 seating configuration, with Chinese people generally being of a smaller stature. Route 30 used to go to Tsuen Wan Ferry bus station, another location which was swept away by the Western Harbour redevelopment.

There was no shortage of variety in the KMB fleet of the early 1980s. Rubbing shoulders with 1950s Daimler CVGs were the likes of No. (3)M2, one of three 12-metre-long three-axle MCW Metrobuses which joined the fleet in 1981. KMB followed up the trial of these buses with orders for eighty-eight 9.7-metre models and 254 11-metre three-axle variants throughout the decade. Route 112 was one of the then recently created Cross-Harbour tunnel routes which saw buses of both CMB and KMB crossing under the harbour.

A scene in Des Voeux Road in central Hong Kong sees two KMB buses on Cross-Harbour routes being pursued by four of HK's famous double-deck tramcars. Duple Met. Sec-bodied Dennis Jubilants Nos N307/15 are seen when virtually brand new in October 1981. Note the farebox, common to many buses in the UK. Route 111 originated in Ping Shek, just north of the now closed Kai Tak International Airport.

In 1985 KMB ordered its first non-British chassis, following the lifting of the 'Imperial Preference' restrictions. Having previously operated a Mercedes 0.305 for trials, a further forty were obtained for use on the long route 68 through the New Territories. The Alexander bodies were shipped out CKD and assembled at the Tuen Mun Works. They were the only buses painted in this attractive livery variation. No. ME18 is seen leaving Jordan Road Ferry bus station in December 1985. (JW)

Yuen Long West bus station still retained very much the same layout in 2018 as it did in 1981. 1961 BACO-bodied Albion Victor No. L67 shows off the tidy back end of the type as it waits to leave on a route 54 journey to Sheung Tsuen (Shek Kong). While the bus was withdrawn in February 1986, route 54 continues to serve the same places to this day.

Metal Sections-bodied Daimler CVG5 No. D250 was new in 1961 and was originally of H65R configuration. The doors were fitted in the mid-1960s while the additional front entrance dates from the mid-1970s. It is seen on the north bank of the Lam Tsuen River in Ting Kok Road in Tai Po on route 75 from nearby Tai Mei Tuk. The river bank is in the process of being strengthened with stone blockwork.

This Daimler CVG6LX-34 in all-over advert colours was somewhat of a rarity. KMB operated a total of 170 of these 34-foot-long Met. Sec-bodied Daimlers, which were received between 1969 and 1972. This model was only available to the export market. No. D361 is seen in Public Square Street on route 3C, which connected the Jordan Road Ferry with Tsz Wan Shan (North). A considerable number of these buses saw further service with Stagecoach in Malawi, following their withdrawal by KMB in 1988/9.

The majority of KMB's Daimler CVG5s were withdrawn between 1979 and 1983, with the last examples lingering on until the early part of 1984. As large numbers of new buses were placed into service in Kowloon, a considerable number of Daimler CVG6s were moved to the New Territory routes. By 1985 Sheung Shui had also gained a new bus station and CVG6s Nos D299/79/310 are seen waiting to leave on local services. These buses were then allocated to Un (Yuen) Long depot. (JW)

In wet weather the buses tend to get very grimy but the KMB answer is to wash them down between duties. With buckets of soapy water at the ready, the bus washer takes a well-earned rest after cleaning Leyland Victory No. G182. Daimler CVG6LX-30 No. D587 is next in line for the wash at Jordan Road Ferry.

Metal Sections-bodied AEC Regent V No. A56 entered service on 29 May 1964 and gave KMB nineteen years of reliable service. They were powered by AEC's trusted AV690 engine unit. As indicated on the Jordan Road Ferry bus station stand board, route 14 served Yau Tong to the east of Kowloon. Note the hot water dispenser alongside the dispatcher's cabin.

This December 1985 view sees Metal Sections-bodied Daimler CVG6 No. D308 leading sister vehicle No. D569 along San Fang Avenue in the centre of Sheung Shui in the New Territories. At 31 feet in length, the latter bus was actually a foot longer than No. D308 and had seven more seats. Both buses would be withdrawn during the next twelve months. This view had hardly changed over the following thirty-three years – only the buses were different. (JW)

A line-up of buses at Sheung Shui garage with Albion Vikings Nos L265/91 rubbing shoulders with 1956 rebuilt Daimler CVG5 No. D115. A number of the CVG5s between Nos D1–150 had what was referred to as the 'Birmingham' grille while Nos D151–260 had what was known as the 'Manchester' grille. No. D115 was withdrawn only two weeks after this picture was taken.

KMB took a leaf out of London Transport's book in that the buses were fitted with sliding cab doors, thus enabling the drivers to get in the cab when they were parked close together. Dennis Jubilants Nos N9 and N43 are the outer layers in a Daimler CVG6 sandwich at Kwun Tong Ferry bus station.

Nathan Road runs south to north through the main commercial district of Kowloon and plays host to a variety of bus services. Heading south are former LT Daimler Fleetline No. 2D35 (ex-DMS1533) and 1967 Met. Sec-bodied Daimler CVG6 No. D348. Route 7 started at Kowloon Tong and terminated at the Star Ferry bus station.

This broadside view of No. D532 gives some indication as to just how big these long Daimler CVG6s were. Introduced between 1969 and 1972, there were 200 of these Met. Sec-bodied ninety-two-seaters, which had a wheelbase of 21 feet 6 inches and an overall length of 34 feet 4½ inches. Originally operated by a crew of two, they were later fitted with fareboxes for OPO operation. No. D532 lasted in service until November 1988, when it was sold to Stagecoach-Malawi.

KMB had a large fleet of older buses attached to the training school, which was located at Sha Tin. Daimler CVG5 No. D29 was one of the oldest buses in the fleet, having first been registered on 1 May 1949. It was withdrawn from the PSV fleet in March 1980. In 1981 the training school basically consisted of an open ground situated alongside the Tai Po Road, opposite the Sha Tin Racecourse which opened in 1978. Now the site of high rise buildings, KMB later relocated to a multi-storey garage on an alternative site on the opposite side of the Shing Mun River.

The training school contained a number of these Daimler CVG5s, which were now painted in this attractive colour scheme. No. 4614 had been No. D197 in the PSV fleet and had been new in 1960. It was withdrawn from public service in February 1982. This view shows it in the developing region of Sha Tin in December 1985. (JW)

Another view of Metal Sections-bodied Daimler CVG5 No. D197. It is seen in Po Yick Street in the centre of Tai Po only four months before it was withdrawn from PSV use. Route 74 was a relatively short route to nearby Sam Mun Tsai. Somewhat difficult to see in the dark shadows on the left is a navvy gang, which entirely comprised women, digging out a trench.

Among the second-hand buses obtained from the UK was a small batch of three Daimler CCG6s which had been new to Chesterfield Corporation in December 1963. They only lasted ten years with Chesterfield before being snapped up by KMB in 1973. While Nos 2D2/3 were withdrawn after three years, No. 2D1 was rebodied and lasted in service until January 1984. It is seen in Kwun Tong Ferry bus station.

The last thirty-four Albion Vikings, Nos L279–312, received forty-nine-seat bodies constructed by United Auto Bodies of HK and entered service in 1976. Other than the last four, they were originally painted in this livery arrangement, which was still carried by No. L297 in 1981. It is seen in Public Square Street in Kowloon on the normally double-deck-worked route 70.

One of the early types of front-engined double-decker buses tried by KMB in the 1970s was the Guy Victory J. Four examples were bodied by BBA/Busaf of Port Elizabeth (SA) and were received in January 1976. On the left, No. G3 is seen in Argyle Street in the Tai Kok Tsui district of Kowloon. On the right, 1969 Met. Sec-bodied Daimler CVG6 No. D563 is seen at Kwun Tong Metro station, which was opened in 1979.

During the 1970s the KMB network expanded at a rapid rate and the company bought a number of British operators' cast off buses. These included Leyland Titans, Atlanteans, Daimlers and AEC Regent Vs. The KMB numbering system used the prefix '2' for all second-hand buses. No. 2A23 was a former Halifax JOC bus which was acquired in 1973 and is seen at Yuen Long depot. It was rebodied in 1976 and withdrawn in March 1982. Note the painter hard at work.

A busy scene in Tai Po Tai Wo Road sees five Albions heading west. 1963 Victor No. L95 is seen on route 73 heading for Man Kam To, near the Chinese border, while 1976 Viking No. L301 is turning out of Ting Kok Road and is heading for Tai Wai. In the distance are two buses on route 64 from Yuen Long, one of which is No. L215.

KMB's remit is to transport large numbers of people over relatively short distances. To this end most of the fleet comprised high-density double-deckers. However, in the mid-1970s they did operate a fleet of 100 forty-two-seater Duple-bodied Albion (Leyland) Viking coaches. BF 3717 is seen heading down Nathan Road on route 246, which ran from the Star Ferry to Lai Yiu. Regent V No. A109 is following behind on route 4.

The early evening sun accentuates the front of 1954 Met. Sec-bodied Daimler CVG5 No. D17 as it stops to set down (note the lettering on the road surface) passengers at Hung Hom railway station. Although it is devoid of a destination blind, it is carrying a slip-board in the front window which denotes the destination in both English and Chinese. No. D17 was withdrawn in March 1983.

Looking every inch a product of W. Alexander's Falkirk factory, 1980-built Dennis Jubilant No. N88 is seen laying over at Kwun Tong Metro station. This was a relatively new bus station, having been opened as an interchange with the newly constructed (1979) Metro line. Note the storm drains set in the adjacent slope to discharge the waters of the monsoon rains.

Former LT MCW-bodied Daimler Fleetline No. DMS1593 joined the KMB fleet as No. 2D31 in May 1981. The most obvious alteration from its LT days is the provision of full-depth sliding windows. It is seen in Kowloon's busy Nathan Road on route 7A from Hung Hom railway station with Met. Sec-bodied Fleetline No. D786 and unnumbered Alexander-bodied Dennis Jubliant double-deck coach CP 4180 in hot pursuit. No. 2D31 later saw service in Tianjin in China.

Another of KMB's venerable Daimler CVG5s is seen at work in the New Territories. Once regarded as mainstream buses in Kowloon, they were ousted from the primary routes by the influx of Guy Victories and Dennis Jubilants. No. D118, which dated from 1956, was over twenty-five years old when seen in Po Heung Street in Tai Po.

When photographed at the Citybus training school in February 1997, No. 4964 was thought to be one of only three surviving members of KMB's once 365-strong fleet of Daimler CVG5s. One of the first to be registered in May 1949, it was eventually numbered D29 and remained in service with KMB until March 1980, when it was transferred to the training school. (PG)

The Sociedade de Transportes Colectivos do Porto S. A. (STCP) was (and still is) the principal operator of road transport in the city of Oporto in Portugal in the 1980s with an interesting collection of buses, trolleybuses and ancient four-wheel trams. Looking every inch like a typical UK bus of the era, No. 226 was one of a batch of thirty Leyland PDR1/1 Atlanteans with locally built Dalfa bodywork which joined the fleet in 1963/4 and is seen in the central district of Carmo in June 1983.

The Dalfa-bodied Atlanteans were followed by a further ninety examples in 1966/7 but these had the rather attractive Salvador Caetano bodywork, another local bodybuilder whose assembly works was situated in Ovar to the south of Oporto. No. 274 is seen in Rua do Infante D. Henrique in the Infante district in April 1982. This scene has since been enhanced by the extension of the STCP heritage tram line alongside the adjacent church.

Forty-five single-deck Leyland Royal Tiger Worldmasters with B38D bodywork by Salvador Caetano were ordered for delivery in 1967/8. Numbered 62–106, they were later renumbered to 462–506 and the majority were rebodied between 1979 and 1981 with UTIC-Porto B29D or B33D capacity bodies. No. 479, still in original form, is seen in Rua de Alexandre Braga in the centre of Oporto in April 1982. It was withdrawn in 1987.

Another of STCP's large intake of Caetano-bodied Atlanteans, No. 313 is seen in Praça de Gomes Teixeira at Carmo in June 1983. These eighty-seven-seater buses were withdrawn around the end of the decade but No. 313 remains in existence and is now part of the collection of buses at the STCP museum in Oporto, having been repainted into its original turquoise and cream livery. 1976 Volvo No. 616 is seen behind.

The STCP depot at Areosa, in the east of the city, was home to both buses and trolleybuses, and although the last trolleybuses were withdrawn in December 1997, it continued as a bus depot until the 2000s before being closed completely. Leyland Tiger Worldmaster No. 476 and Atlantean No. 285 rest between duties at Areosa depot in April 1982. Note the trolleybus wires and the depot name above the fleet numbers.

Dalfa-bodied Leyland Atlantean No. 231 is seen negotiating the large roundabout at Boavista. Behind the bus is one of STCP's ancient four-wheel tramcars, the earliest of which, still in use at the time, dated from 1909. In the background is the Monumento aos Heróis da Guerra Peninsular (Heroes of the Peninsular War of 1808–14).

Proudly displaying its Atlantean badge, even after seventeen years of service with STCP, No. 275 waits to depart Carmo on service 78 to the coast. Similar bus No. 321 waits behind on another local city route. Oporto was the only municipal operator to use buses which combined the Atlantean chassis with Salvador Caetano bodywork – the result was both stylish and unique.

Boavista was the location of the main tram depot. However, by 1982 the tram system had been cut to just four routes and consequently some of the space previously used by the trams was turned over to the overhaul of both buses and trolleybuses. Caetano-bodied Leyland Atlantean No. 256 is minus most of its glazing as it undergoes a full repaint.

Leyland Royal Tiger Worldmaster No. 506 (originally No. 106) was rebodied by UTIC-Porto in January 1980, having originally carried a Caetano body. It is seen in Rua de Gonçalo Cristovão in April 1982. Again, the Royal Tiger badge is prominent on the front, as is the depot name above the fleet number. It lasted in service until 1995.

An evocative view of the north bank of the River Douro sees one of the Caetano-bodied Atlanteans in Avenida de Gustavo Eiffel heading out to Alfandega on route 88. The bus is about to pass under the spectacular Ponte Luiz I bridge, which in 1982 carried trolleybuses across the upper span and buses on the lower level. The upper deck has since been converted to a metro line. A lone figure at a doorway watches the bus go by.

Another view inside the Boavista works sees Dalfa-bodied Leyland Atlantean No. 230 and Lancia trolleybus No. 145 also receiving a heavy overhaul. Note how the trolleybuses retained their grey roof after repainting into orange and cream. Boavista ceased to be used as a tram depot after 1988 and was closed completely in 1999. The building was razed to the ground and a concert hall has since been built on the site.

STCP operated trolleybuses between 1959 and 1997, when the last remnants of the system were closed. The fleet was largely made up of both single and double-deck Lancias. However, the first twenty-six were Leyland LETB/1s with UTIC-Lisboa bodywork. This model was based on BUT technology while the bodies were of a Park Royal design. Nos 11 and 4, both new in 1959 and painted in the attractive red and grey livery, are seen at the Bolhao terminus in the centre of Oporto in June 1983.

The Oporto trolleybus system wasn't particularly extensive but most of the routes operated penetrated out into the surrounding countryside. Leyland LETB/1 No. 22 was one of an additional six of the type which were obtained in 1963. They differed from the first twenty in that they had three entrances and only twenty seats. It is seen in Rua Rodrigues de Freitas, having just left the small town of Ermesinde. Single-deckers were a necessity on this route as it is about to pass under a bridge with a 4.0-metre headroom.

STCP services 33, 35 and 36 were tramway replacement services which commenced running to Vila Nova de Gaia in 1959. They were operated by trolleybuses until July 1993 but this April 1982 view sees Leyland Tiger Worldmaster No. 491 in Rua de Sá Da Bandeira working on service 33 to Coimbrões, on the outskirts of Vila Nova de Gaia.

Another UTIC-Porto rebodied Worldmaster, No. 481, is seen rounding a bend in Rua Rodrigues de Freitas at Alto da Maia in April 1982. It is heading back to Oporto city centre. Note the trolleybus wires, which were used by service 9 to Ermesinde. The same location presented a different view in 2018, as not only had the wires long since been removed (in 1994) but the stone setts had also been replaced by tarmacadam.

Route 78 terminated in Praça de Gonçalves Zarco at Castelo do Quejo, overlooking the Atlantic Ocean. The Praça was a large roundabout situated at the end of the dead straight Avenida da Boavista, some 3.2 miles from the Boavista tram depot, and was partly encircled by three of the remaining four tram routes (note the overhead wires). It would appear that the STCP driver has abandoned Atlantean No. 301 in the middle of the road as it waits to return to the São Joao Hospital. Inset: The view from the top deck – what remained of the oil tanker *Jacob Maersk*, which ran aground on 29 January 1975.

The first ten Leyland Worldmasters, Nos 452–61, joined the STCP fleet in 1960 and had bodies constructed by Dalfa. No. 454 is seen in Rua de Gonçalo Cristovão and is still sporting the turquoise and ivory livery first introduced in 1960. The last two of the decemvirate were withdrawn in 1985. Lancia trolleybus No. 130 can be seen in the background turning out of Rua de Santa Catarina. The tram lines were last used by route 7 in June 1977, some five years prior to this photograph being taken.

Former London Routemasters could be seen all over the world once they had been discarded by the capital city. No. RMA5 was new to British European Airways (BEA) in 1967. It was acquired by LT in 1975 and passed to Stagecoach East London in 1994. It is seen on tour at Ribeira de Sintra in Portugal, alongside the Sintra Tramway Depot where Car No. 4 is reposing, in April 1999. The line was originally opened in 1904. (PG)

Ashok Motors of India was formed in 1948 and in 1954 the company obtained a license to manufacture the Leyland Comet. A version of the PD3/5 followed in 1967 which evolved into the ALPD in 1984. These buses were still being built, although not in half-cab form, well into the twenty-first century. Brihanmumbai Electric Supply & Transport (BEST) No. 4782 is seen in Hornby Road in the centre of Mumbai (Bombay). (JW)

The Ashok Leyland Viking was a prolific model which was introduced by the Indian bus builder in 1976. Whereas most of the BEST double-deckers carried advert liveries (as illustrated in the background) the Vikings were almost universally turned out in the fleet colours of red and grey. No. 5964 is seen negotiating the Flora Fountain traffic system in the centre of Mumbai. The impressive-looking building behind is known as the Oriental Buildings and dates from 1885. (JW)

Another busy scene at Flora Fountain depicts ALPD No. 4780 turning into Veer Nariman Road. Two more Indian Titans and two Vikings can be seen in the background. Although dating from the 1990s, the design had hardly changed from its inception in 1967. There were still over a hundred of the type in service in Mumbai in 2018. (JW)

A classic rear view of a BEST ALPD features No. 4765 at Colaba bus station. Note the letters Bb after the number, which denotes the depot code – in this case Back Bay. Back Bay was one of five central area depots, which also included Colaba. The fleet number was only displayed in Hindu-Arabic numerals on the back of the buses while all lettering on the front, including the fleet and route number, was shown in Hindi. (JW)

A line up of ALPDs, the first two of which are Nos 4731/67, are seen parked up on the west side of Churchgate railway station. Along with CST (Chhatrapati Shivaji Maharaj Terminus), Churchgate was one of two terminal stations in central Mumbai which served the extremely busy suburban rail network. (JW)

Two Ashok Leyland Vikings, Nos 8230 and 7400, are seen in Mararshi Karve Road on the east side of Churchgate railway station. For over thirty years the city fleet was largely made up of numerous examples of this Indian workhorse. The Viking was available with a variety of internal layouts consisting of between forty-two and fifty-eight seats in a 2+2 or 2+3 formation. One drawback was the three-step entrance, which on later models was modified to two steps. (JW)

One of the more prestigious orders (at the time) won by Leyland was to supply eight Atlanteans to the Metropolitan Transport Authority of New York City in 1976. With bodywork by Park Royal in the Mancunian style, they were not a great success and were restricted to certain routes due to their height. In 1980 all eight buses were bought by Gray Line, who used them on sightseeing tours in San Francisco. No. 405 is seen at Union Square in August 1982. They later worked in Victoria in British Columbia, Canada.

Over twenty ECW-bodied Bristol LHs from a variety of UK operators were shipped out to Malta. This forty-three-seat model had been new to Hants & Dorset in January 1975 as No. 3553. It had entered service in Malta by 1986 and was put aside for preservation following its withdrawal in 2011. Looking immaculately turned out, it is seen at Valletta bus terminal in March 2007. The 'Leyland' name seems somewhat inappropriate. (PG)

For many years the buses in Malta were operated by owner-drivers who went to great lengths to customise their vehicles. In the early 1980s and later, around sixty of London Transport's AEC Swifts were exported to Malta. This Park Royal-bodied bus was formerly SMS237 and is seen at Sliema Ferry on the north coast of the island. (PG)

Former LT AEC Swift SMS603 did not go out to Malta until May 1992. When photographed at Valletta bus station in March 2002 it was owned by Leon Grech of Paramount garage at Mosta. Looking pristine in the later universal yellow and white livery, the front has been somewhat altered and it carries an AEC badge. It was withdrawn and scrapped in 2011. (PG)

In its London Transport days, SMS275 had first operated out of Elmers End garage and worked on route 194. When in service in Malta barely two of the Swifts looked the same following the different alterations made by their owners. FBY 756 is seen at Mater Dei Hospital in Valletta in March 2002. (PG)

London's AEC Swifts had been bodied by a number of coachbuilders – namely Marshall, MCW and Park Royal. There was also a mixture of single and dual-door vehicles. No prizes for guessing which type of body former LT SM9 carried. FBY 738 arrived in Malta in May 1981 and was originally painted in the green and white livery. Like all the other owner-vehicles, it was withdrawn in 2011 following the disastrous takeover of the island's bus services by Arriva. It is seen at Valletta bus station in October 2006. (PG)

A number of London's Swifts were used by the Government Education Department of Malta as school transport buses. What had been SMS356 is seen in the department's purplish blue and greyish cream livery resting at the Floriana Parking Area in Valletta in April 2001. It had arrived in Malta in 1980 and was reported as stored at Cancu in 2015. When photographed it was completely unmodified and retained its LT configuration both inside and out, including its turnstile gate. (PG)

Three Leyland Lynxes from the Preston Bus fleet were shipped over to Malta in 2007/8. The former Nos 211/3 had been new to Preston in March 1989 and joined the Malta fleet in March 2007. DBY 379 (No. 213) was owned by Saviour Grech of Mquabba and is seen in Sliema in 2009. The third vehicle, No. 226, never actually operated in Malta. (PG)

No. RMF 588 was operated by the Cancu Bus Service Company, based in the town of Zetjun in Malta, in May 2008. COY 004 began life as Northern General No. 2118 (FPT 588C) in February 1965 (renumbered to 3102 in 1975). After withdrawal by Northern in 1978 it operated sightseeing tours in London before being converted to open-top format in 1987. It was subsequently owned by Blue Triangle, the Big Bus Co. and Ensignbus before being exported to Malta in March 2007. It is seen close to its Cancu base. (PG)

City sightseeing tours are big business the world over. The Big Bus Company was one of a number of tourist bus companies offering open-top bus rides in the United Arab Emirates. Former London Transport Leyland Titan No. T362 and New World First Bus (ex-CMB) Dennis Condor No. DA6 are seen in Deira City in Dubai in November 2010. (PG)

In 1968/9 the Istanbul Electric Tram & Tunnel Company (IETT) took delivery of a large order of thirty-six-seater MCW-bodied Leyland EL3.45/37 Olympics (or Levends as they were known in Turkey), comprising no fewer than 300 vehicles. No. 916, looking somewhat battered and bruised, is seen at the Istanbul Ferry Terminal bus station in April 1985.

The New Lantau Bus Co. was formed in 1973 and the initial fleet was essentially made up of buses from the island's previous operators, which included the United Lantau Bus Co. Ltd and the Ngong Ping Bus Co. These were added to throughout the 1970s and the fleet mainly consisted of Commer, Dodge and Fargo makes, which were all essentially made by the same company. In among the plethora of single-deckers at the Pui O depot in October 1981 is 1980 Alexander-bodied Leyland Victory CC 9088.

NLB BE 5441 was a Commer RG13 with a B38F Sun Cheong Auto Body which was new in 1973. It was one of twelve of the type operated by the company. Commer was founded in Luton in 1905 and becamc part of the Rootes Group in 1931. The Dodge/Fargo name replaced the Commer name following the takeover of the Rootes Group by Chyrsler in the mid-1970s. Commer finally ceased production in 1979. BE 5441 is seen on South Lantau Road descending the hill into Pui O on route 1 to Tai O.

Only three of these small Dodge KC40s were operated by NLB and they were an ideal bus to operate along the narrow twisty road to Ngong Ping and the Po Lin Monastery. New in 1979, they had a twenty-five-seat body constructed by the Sun Cheong Auto Body Co. The Dodge is seen at the entrance to the monastery, which was founded in 1906.

When visited in October 1981, the NLB Company had recently taken delivery of a further four of these Alexander-bodied Leyland Victory megadeckers. Three more were to follow in 1982/3, bringing the total operated up to nine. One of the two 1980 examples, CC 9897, is seen basking in the sun at Silvermine Bay. At the time the open-air depot was situated a few miles to the west, along the coast at Pui O.

NLB went on to operate a fleet of fifteen Leyland Victories, with six more examples being purchased second-hand from KMB between 1985 and 1991. However, problems were experienced with the type and ten of them were sold to Citybus in 1993. One of the remaining five, No. LD5 (CP 3655), is seen in the later fleet colours at Mui Wo (Silvermine Bay) bus station in February 1997. (PG)

Unitrans was founded in 1968, as the University Transport System, when the Associated Students of University College Davis (USA) purchased two 'vintage' ex-LT double-decker buses to operate two routes. The operational fleet eventually comprised six RTs (plus three for spares) and two RTLs. Five of the RTs were still owned in 2017, including No. RT4735, which had been fitted with a Cummins engine and was still considered to be part of the active fleet. It is seen on the university campus in October 1992. (JW)

This Roe-bodied Daimler CRG6LX was new to the West Riding Automobile Co. as No. 212 in May 1969. Not only is it still displaying its UK registration plate but the 6773 is a reference to its Daimler chassis number, this being 62773. No. 213 was also acquired by Unitrans. It was noted as semi-derelict at Mayville in New York State in mid-2008. This view again dates from October 1992. (JW)

Park Royal-bodied No. RTL1014 entered service with London Transport in July 1950. Withdrawn in June 1967, it was exported to the USA three months later where it joined the fledgling Unitrans bus fleet at the University of California in Davis. It was finally retired from active duty in December 2007 and placed in store. It returned to the UK in January 2012 and is now part of the Ensignbus heritage fleet. It is seen at the university in October 1996. (JW)

Argos Bus of Hong Kong was established in 1981 to transport workers at the China Shipbuilding Company to and from their homes in the urban areas. The fleet was largely made up of former LT and West Midlands PTE Fleetlines. No. 54 was an ex-WMPTE bus while No. 32 behind had worked for London Transport. They are seen in central Hong Kong in November 1990. The company now operates a fleet of luxury coaches. (JW)

Citybus of Hong Kong began with very humble beginnings and was founded in August 1979 by a former CMB employee. By 1981 the company was operating a service from central Hong Kong to the Ocean Park animal theme park, which had opened in 1977. The moderately sized fleet mainly comprised former British operators' Daimler Fleetlines. Former Bournemouth Transport Alexander-bodied No. 188 is depicted in October 1981.

A trio of Citybus Fleetlines is seen parked up at Ocean Park. They are former Bournemouth Transport Alexander-bodied No. 191, former London Transport MCW-bodied No. DM1749 and Park Royal-bodied No. DMS788. Throughout the 1980s the company went from strength to strength, so much so that they gained a large number of franchised routes from CMB in 1993. It is now a subsidiary of New World First Bus, the principal operator of bus services on the island of Hong Kong in 2018.

Another former London Transport Fleetline in the Citybus fleet was No. DMS796. It became the first double-deck bus to visit China in over fifty years when it was taken to the border town of Shenzhen in December 1981. After ten years' service with Citybus it was sold to the Guangzhou No. 1 Bus Company in China. The bus behind is former Eastern National Bristol FLF No. 2928, which was new in 1968. It was shipped to HK in July 1981 and was later converted to an open-top bus.

As Citybus expanded over the years and eventually won a significant number of route franchises from CMB, they continued to cater for the tourist market. Three former LT Routemasters were operated by the company; all were heavily rebuilt and converted to open-top format. Former No. RM1288 of 1962 and No. 1 in the Citybus fleet is seen at Siu Sai Wan bus station in October 1998. (PG)

The Guangzhou No. 1 Bus Company started operating double-decker buses on a regular basis in 1987. The company purchased a number of former KMB buses including Daimler CVG6s and former LT Daimler Fleetlines. More of the latter were also obtained from Citybus. No. 3-1-513 (LT identity unknown) is seen on route 269 in October 1998 – this was the last year double-deckers operated on Guangzhou's city routes. (PG)

This ECW-bodied Bristol MW was chanced upon in the Chinese town of Shenzhen in October 1981. The arrangement of the destination and route apertures suggests that it may have begun life with the Bristol Omnibus Co. Furthermore, three former BOC MWs, namely HAE 261/4/5D, were reported as being exported to the Far East in 1980. With a population of around 35,000 at the time, Shenzhen has now grown to a city of 11 million and is where BYD, the world's largest manufacturers of electric buses, is based.

Acknowledgements

The author would like to thank Jeff Watson (JW) and Peter Gascoine (PG) for the use of some of their images in the compilation of this book and these are denoted as shown. All other images are the copyright of the author.

Bibliography

Brown, Stewart, *Daimler Buses in Camera*, (London: Ian Allan Ltd, 1978).

Davis, Mike, *Hong Kong Buses Volume One – China Motor Bus*, (Croydon: DTS Publishing, 1994).

Davis, Mike, *Hong Kong Buses Volume Two – Kowloon Motor Bus*, (Croydon: DTS Publishing, 1995).

Jack, Doug, *Leyland Bus Mk 2*, (Glossop: Transport Publishing Company, 1984).

Manning, Ian, *Portuguese Buses Volume Two – Cities & Municipalities*, (Croydon: DTS Publishing, 2007).

Pettie, Jasper, *Guy Buses in Camera*, (London: Ian Alan Ltd, 1979).

PSV Circle Fleet Histories WWK4, WWK5 & WWK7 (Buses in South Africa)